# Moments in Silence

Ravi Kommarraju

Presentation by *BookLeaf Publishing*

Web: www.bookleafpub.com

E-mail: info@bookleafpub.com

ISBN: 9789360942823

First edition 2024

To my Gurus

# ACKNOWLEDGEMENT


To the great mystic Masters

# PREFACE

Silence talks.  In sublime moments a rhythm resonates inside, loudly echoing tones that cannot be heard by ears.  Hasn't' Keats said the same "heard memories are sweet, those unheard are sweeter still"?  These metamorphose sometimes into words and sentences. Can they catch the silent sounds?  Can these convey an untold story?  Can a mysterious invisible imagery draw itself and etch its shadows in amorphous colours that can mutate into sounds? Perhaps it does in some fleeting moments of pregnant silence.  Such moments have visited me, knocking on the doors of my heart, whispering shared meanings of floating silences. I recorded some, some just resonate and come back to greet and gently touch to remind. Perhaps I will record them too at another moment or later.  They exist immortaly in on ethereal orbit and are never lost.  Catch them if you can when they pass by.  You only need to listen to the meandering music of sublime silence.

Here are some of those moments of silence.  Savour them with your heart.
Ravi Komarraju

# Monalisa

She forgot to laugh out loud
In the cavernous halls of loneliness
When a painter came along with a child
She smiled gently, Mona Lisa!

# Rainbow

2

Why do you hide in the light?
Is it only possible in ecstasy,
To break free in tears of joy
Rainbow in the sky?!

# The Bee

3

Why should I wonder for just seven buildings?
Built by slaves or grieving labour?
Why shouldn't I wonder when a million bees
Build a hive for honey to store?
A toil for their joy and for millions of people too?!

# Waterless

The summer is hot and scorching
Taps don't dribble, there's nothing in the pond
Cities with Babel towers have no drop to drink
Fly away little birds to where water brings.

# War & Hope

5

How can you build a joyous city on the perched
hand of tears?
How can the echoes of laughter be real in a
desolate shattered dream wars fires have broken
the hearths of a million homes?
A soulless ambition had blew out the lights of
hope.
How many hands can wipe the little cheeks?
Which empire or god can bring life to the dead?
Maybe we can nurture a wild flower in a
hardened rock crevice.
Maybe a drop of love somewhere will let it
sprout somehow!
Perhaps, maybe!!! Maybe !!

# Driving on the highways

You can't run across the i70 west
Unless you are a foolish frightened deer
I am my machine and my map
I am a foolish sheep following my peer.

# The Cocktail

Life has been a strange admixture
Of the known and unknown,
A cocktail of illusion and reality
Of a shout and an echo
Of endless Time and Space.

Life has always everywhere been
A Prism's deflected beam
A moonlit Ocean's gleam
Ever percolating down darkness unseen.

Life has always been everywhere
A ceaseless quest through ages
A dazzling Aurora Borealis
A sweet, deep, intoxicating, melancholy.

# The Bee

The foraging bee never knew
There was poison in the air
And that flowers can be deadly too
And after it sucked the honey, it never flew!!

# What we lost

9

He lazed in the sun and got Vitamin D
He roamed in the forest and was free
Tell me the law and I'll let you see
Where shackles don't touch you and me

# Morning Coffee

It's a small small world brother
Picked up and roasted brown
All soils end up in lather
In the little coffee cup, my own.

# Life



For once, I loved to live
When I saw, a flower bloom

# The echo

Somewhere my soul wants to lie
Sing a rhythm with the flower
Dance with the lily on water
And dissolve in dew!
Somewhere my 'being' desires to
Beat my heart with thunder
Fly-out aloud with the echo
And vanish in the clouds!

# What if

What if "AI" says 'IAM'
My face is a number
My voice becomes a copy
Our planet a divided matrix
For control freak soulless leaders
Roads, streets, houses, hotels just clicking
cameras
What if today and tomorrow
Are timeliness for machines
What if teaching is not learning
Just an enhanced chip hearing?
What if life is just physics and Math?
And biology just alphabet
What if the Earth's Alpha is a vibrating Binary
prefix
What if life becomes criss-crossed lines?
For whom should the flowers blossom or the
Moon ride the waves?

# Coffee Cup

The bulb was a blob
Broken rings of light
Moving in the lather
Of my coffee cup!

# An Old Garland

Hanging on the wall
It had a story to tell
It had in its heart a temple bell
Wafting memories in its flowery smell

# The Beep

I know it so well
Even in my sleep
No, not the unknown bird's chirp
It's just the damn car's beep!

# My Mobile

A history in hand
All the world's happenings
Almost my entire life
Rings often in my hand

# Plastic

How strange that coal
Can be transparent
Fill the oceans and the placenta
Remain a million years
To tell a tale of man's failure

# Insects



Who says insects are dumb
That they just vanish away
Remember they haven't a weapon built
For a Total War!!

# A Remnant

A relic of the past
Man's intelligent friend
His slow-flowing recorder
The ever-faithful old pen!

# Redwoods

It was a thousand hands praying
Breathing out breathing in
It was a thousand soldiers defending
A last bastion from following
These redwoods that we have

# The rainbow

Myriad colours are the magic of life
A green little twig sprouts a resplendent rose
To seekers of everything precious, nature opens
itself
Isn't it from little seeds that mighty redwoods
arose?
On an azure rainy sky
The sun painted a rainbow
Colours locked in the blinding light of its core
What matters if it's a mosque or temple or
grotto?
Nature's hues merge and vanish in light all the
more.
To a bee a lotus, to a butterfly a jasmine
To a poet a daffodil, to the little maid a hibiscus
Small passions and love for scents,
Colours and sounds so human
To mind's eye forms are only for a focus
Truth is brighter and clearer than the sun
The rainbow, my friend, is only a wondrous
reflection.

# The moon

The moon is like the early morning sun draped
in dew
Like a pink-purple ball kicked into the eastern
sky
On the shadowy contours of Herculean
Palmyrahs—Globe-like !
A distance like in a dark tunnel of a coal field
Feebly focusing on the sea and a passing ship
A drizzling aphrodisiac on the beach
A soothing balm to a gaping world
A music and a song from the east to the west

# Time's Wink

That time that glided in an eye wink
Flew without wings
The world was born
An vanished in an instant
How many universes have been born?
How many had melted away
Every day, every minute,
I just can't say

# In Darkness and light

25

Beyond those mountains no one lives
My home is the best
And my chair most heavenly
I gloated
Somewhere beyond the blue horizon
Far away near waves like these
Someone might be thinking just like me